I0016531

FORWARD/COMMENTARY

The National Institute of Standards and Technology (NIST) is a measurement standards laboratory, and a non-regulatory agency of the **United States Department of Commerce**. Its mission is to promote innovation and industrial competitiveness. Founded in 1901, as the National Bureau of Standards, NIST was formed with the mandate to provide standard weights and measures, and to serve as the national physical laboratory for the United States. With a world-class measurement and testing laboratory encompassing a wide range of areas of computer science, mathematics, statistics, and systems engineering, NIST's cybersecurity program supports its overall mission to promote U.S. innovation and industrial competitiveness by advancing measurement science, standards, and related technology through research and development in ways that enhance economic security and improve our quality of life.

The need for cybersecurity standards and best practices that address interoperability, usability and privacy has been shown to be critical for the nation. NIST's cybersecurity programs seek to enable greater development and application of practical, innovative security technologies and methodologies that enhance the country's ability to address current and future computer and information security challenges.

The cybersecurity publications produced by NIST cover a wide range of cybersecurity concepts that are carefully designed to work together to produce a holistic approach to cybersecurity primarily for government agencies and constitute the best practices used by industry. This holistic strategy to cybersecurity covers the gamut of security subjects from development of secure encryption standards for communication and storage of information while at rest, to how best to recover from a cyber-attack.

Why buy a book you can download for free? We print these books so you don't have to.

Some books are available only in electronic media and you need a hard copy. So, you have to print it yourself – not always easy when you share a LAN printer with 100 other people.

We at 4th Watch Books are former government employees, so we know how people actually use these standards. When a new standard is released, an engineer prints it out, punches holes and puts it in a 3-ring binder. While this is not a big deal for a 5 or 10-page document, many work documents are over 100 pages and printing a large document is a time-consuming effort. An engineer that's paid $75 an hour could spend hours simply printing out the tools needed to do the job. That's time that could be better spent doing engineering. We publish these documents so engineers can focus on what they were hired to do – engineering. It's much more cost-effective to simply order the latest version from Amazon.com. If you like the service we provide, please leave positive review on Amazon so we can continue to print books you need. If there is a standard you would like to see printed, let us know. Our web site is Cybah.webplus.net

See a list of all the docs we print on our CyberSecurity Standards Library™ DVD.

NIST Special Publication 800-40
Revision 3

Guide to Enterprise Patch Management Technologies

Murugiah Souppaya
Karen Scarfone

COMPUTER SECURITY

National Institute of
Standards and Technology
U.S. Department of Commerce

NIST Special Publication 800-40
Revision 3

Guide to Enterprise Patch Management Technologies

Murugiah Souppaya
Computer Security Division
Information Technology Laboratory

Karen Scarfone
Scarfone Cybersecurity
Clifton, VA

July 2013

U.S. Department of Commerce
Penny Pritzker, Secretary

National Institute of Standards and Technology
Patrick D. Gallagher, Under Secretary of Commerce for Standards and Technology and Director

Authority

This publication has been developed by NIST to further its statutory responsibilities under the Federal Information Security Management Act (FISMA), Public Law (P.L.) 107-347. NIST is responsible for developing information security standards and guidelines, including minimum requirements for Federal information systems, but such standards and guidelines shall not apply to national security systems without the express approval of appropriate Federal officials exercising policy authority over such systems. This guideline is consistent with the requirements of the Office of Management and Budget (OMB) Circular A-130, Section 8b(3), *Securing Agency Information Systems*, as analyzed in Circular A-130, Appendix IV: *Analysis of Key Sections*. Supplemental information is provided in Circular A-130, Appendix III, *Security of Federal Automated Information Resources*.

Nothing in this publication should be taken to contradict the standards and guidelines made mandatory and binding on Federal agencies by the Secretary of Commerce under statutory authority. Nor should these guidelines be interpreted as altering or superseding the existing authorities of the Secretary of Commerce, Director of the OMB, or any other Federal official. This publication may be used by nongovernmental organizations on a voluntary basis and is not subject to copyright in the United States. Attribution would, however, be appreciated by NIST.

National Institute of Standards and Technology Special Publication 800-40 Revision 3
Natl. Inst. Stand. Technol. Spec. Publ. 800-40 Rev. 3, 26 pages (July 2013)
http://dx.doi.org/10.6028/NIST.SP.800-40r3
CODEN: NSPUE2

Certain commercial entities, equipment, or materials may be identified in this document in order to describe an experimental procedure or concept adequately. Such identification is not intended to imply recommendation or endorsement by NIST, nor is it intended to imply that the entities, materials, or equipment are necessarily the best available for the purpose.

There may be references in this publication to other publications currently under development by NIST in accordance with its assigned statutory responsibilities. The information in this publication, including concepts and methodologies, may be used by Federal agencies even before the completion of such companion publications. Thus, until each publication is completed, current requirements, guidelines, and procedures, where they exist, remain operative. For planning and transition purposes, Federal agencies may wish to closely follow the development of these new publications by NIST.

Organizations are encouraged to review all draft publications during public comment periods and provide feedback to NIST. All NIST Computer Security Division publications, other than the ones noted above, are available at http://csrc.nist.gov/publications.

Comments on this publication may be submitted to:

National Institute of Standards and Technology
Attn: Computer Security Division, Information Technology Laboratory
100 Bureau Drive (Mail Stop 8930) Gaithersburg, MD 20899-8930

Reports on Computer Systems Technology

The Information Technology Laboratory (ITL) at the National Institute of Standards and Technology (NIST) promotes the U.S. economy and public welfare by providing technical leadership for the Nation's measurement and standards infrastructure. ITL develops tests, test methods, reference data, proof of concept implementations, and technical analyses to advance the development and productive use of information technology. ITL's responsibilities include the development of management, administrative, technical, and physical standards and guidelines for the cost-effective security and privacy of other than national security-related information in Federal information systems. The Special Publication 800-series reports on ITL's research, guidelines, and outreach efforts in information system security, and its collaborative activities with industry, government, and academic organizations.

Abstract

Patch management is the process for identifying, acquiring, installing, and verifying patches for products and systems. Patches correct security and functionality problems in software and firmware. There are several challenges that complicate patch management. If organizations do not overcome these challenges, they will be unable to patch systems effectively and efficiently, leading to easily preventable compromises. This publication is designed to assist organizations in understanding the basics of enterprise patch management technologies. It explains the importance of patch management and examines the challenges inherent in performing patch management. This publication also provides an overview of enterprise patch management technologies and briefly discusses metrics for measuring the technologies' effectiveness and for comparing the relative importance of patches.

Keywords

information security; patch management; remediation; software patches; vulnerability management

Acknowledgments

The authors, Murugiah Souppaya of the National Institute of Standards and Technology (NIST) and Karen Scarfone of Scarfone Cybersecurity, wish to thank their colleagues who reviewed drafts of this document and contributed to its technical content, particularly Peter Mell of NIST.

Acknowledgments, Version 2

The authors, Peter Mell of NIST, Tiffany Bergeron of The MITRE Corporation, and David Henning of Hughes Network Systems, LLC, wish to express their thanks to Rob Pate of the United States Computer Emergency Readiness Team (US-CERT) for providing support for this publication. In addition, the authors would like to thank Miles Tracy of the U.S. Federal Reserve System, who co-authored the original version of the publication and provided significant input for this version, and Tanyette Miller of Booz Allen Hamilton, who put together the patching resources found in the appendices. The authors would also like to express their thanks to Timothy Grance of NIST, Manuel Costa and Todd Wittbold of The MITRE Corporation, Matthew Baum of the Corporation for National and Community Service, and Karen Kent of Booz Allen Hamilton for their insightful reviews, and to representatives from Department of Health and Human Services, Department of State, Environmental Protection Agency, Federal Reserve Board, and PatchAdvisor for their particularly valuable comments and suggestions.

Trademark Information

Microsoft and Windows are either registered trademarks or trademarks of Microsoft Corporation in the United States and other countries.

All other names are registered trademarks or trademarks of their respective companies.

Table of Contents

List of Appendices

Executive Summary

Patch management is the process for identifying, acquiring, installing, and verifying patches for products and systems. Patches correct security and functionality problems in software and firmware. From a security perspective, patches are most often of interest because they are mitigating software flaw vulnerabilities; applying patches to eliminate these vulnerabilities significantly reduces the opportunities for exploitation. Patches serve other purposes than just fixing software flaws; they can also add new features to software and firmware, including security capabilities.

There are several challenges that complicate patch management. Organizations that do not overcome these challenges will be unable to patch systems effectively and efficiently, leading to compromises that were easily preventable. Organizations that can minimize the time they spend dealing with patching can use those resources for addressing other security concerns. Already many organizations have largely operationalized their patch management, making it more of a core IT function than a part of security. However, it is still important for all organizations to carefully consider patch management in the context of security because patch management is so important to achieving and maintaining sound security.

This publication is designed to assist organizations in understanding the basics of enterprise patch management technologies. It explains the importance of patch management and examines the challenges inherent in performing patch management. The publication also provides an overview of enterprise patch management technologies and briefly discusses metrics for measuring the technologies' effectiveness and for comparing the relative importance of patches.

Organizations should implement the following recommendations to improve the effectiveness and efficiency of their enterprise patch management technologies.

Organizations should deploy enterprise patch management tools using a phased approach.

This approach allows process and user communication issues to be addressed with a small group before deploying the patch application universally. Most organizations deploy patch management tools first to standardized desktop systems and single-platform server farms of similarly configured servers. Once this has been accomplished, organizations should address the more difficult issue of integrating multiplatform environments, nonstandard desktop systems, legacy computers, and computers with unusual configurations. Manual methods may need to be used for operating systems and applications not supported by automated patching tools, as well as some computers with unusual configurations.

Organizations should reduce the risks associated with enterprise patch management tools through the application of standard security techniques that should be used when deploying any enterprise-wide application.

Deploying enterprise patch management tools within an enterprise can create additional security risks for an organization; however, a much greater risk is faced by organizations that do not effectively patch their systems. Such tools usually increase security far more than they decrease security, especially when the tools contain built-in security measures to protect against security risks and threats. Risk associated with these tools include patches being altered, credentials being misused, vulnerabilities in the tools being exploited, and entities monitoring tool communications to identify vulnerabilities. Examples of possible countermeasures to these risks include keeping the patching solution components tightly secured and up-to-date, encrypting network communications, verifying the integrity of patches before installing them, and testing patches before deployment.

Organizations should balance their security needs with their needs for usability and availability.

For example, installing a patch may "break" other applications; this can best be addressed by testing patches before deployment. Another example is that forcing application restarts, operating system reboots, and other host state changes is disruptive and could cause loss of data or services. Again, organizations need to balance the need to get patches applied with the need to support operations. A final example, particularly important for mobile devices, is the acquisition of updates over low-bandwidth or metered connections; it may be technically or financially infeasible to download large patches over such connections. Organizations should make provisions for ensuring that their enterprise patching solution works for mobile hosts and other hosts used on low-bandwidth or metered networks.

1. Introduction

1.1 Document Purpose and Scope

This publication is designed to assist organizations in understanding the basics of enterprise patch management technologies. This publication is based on the assumption that the organization has a mature patch management capability and is focused on increasing its automation level. Organizations that are seeking more basic guidance on establishing patch management programs or have legacy needs that cannot be met with current enterprise patch management technologies should, in addition to reading this publication, also consult the previous complementary version, NIST SP 800-40 Version 2, *Creating a Patch and Vulnerability Management Program.*[1]

1.2 Audience

This document has been created for security managers, engineers, administrators, and others who are responsible for acquiring, testing, prioritizing, implementing, and verifying security patches. Auditors and others who need to assess the security of systems may also find this publication useful.

1.3 Document Structure

This document is organized into the following sections and appendices:

- Section 2 explains the importance of patch management.

- Section 3 examines the challenges inherent in performing patch management.

- Section 4 provides an overview of enterprise patch management technologies.

- Section 5 briefly discusses possible metrics for measuring the effectiveness of patch management technologies and for comparing the relative importance of patches.

- Appendix A provides a tutorial on the Security Content Automation Protocol (SCAP) and its role in enterprise patch management.

- Appendix B provides a summary of the main recommendations made throughout the publication.

- Appendix C defines selected acronyms and other abbreviations for the document.

---

[1]   http://csrc.nist.gov/publications/nistpubs/800-40-Ver2/SP800-40v2.pdf

2. The Importance of Patch Management

Patch management is the process for identifying, acquiring, installing, and verifying patches for products and systems. Patches correct security and functionality problems in software and firmware. From a security perspective, patches are most often of interest because they are mitigating software flaw vulnerabilities; applying patches to eliminate these vulnerabilities significantly reduces the opportunities for exploitation. Also, patches are usually the most effective way to mitigate software flaw vulnerabilities, and are often the only fully effective solution. Sometimes there are alternatives to patches, such as temporary workarounds involving software or security control reconfiguration, but these workarounds often negatively impact functionality.

Patches serve other purposes than just fixing software flaws; they can also add new features to software and firmware, including security capabilities. New features can also be added through upgrades, which bring software or firmware to a newer version in a much broader change than just applying a patch. Upgrades may also fix security and functionality problems in previous versions of software and firmware. Also, vendors often stop supporting older versions of their products, which includes no longer releasing patches to address new vulnerabilities, thus making older unsupported versions less secure over time. Upgrades are then necessary to get such products to a supported version that is patched and that has ongoing support for patching newly discovered vulnerabilities.

As Section 3 explains, there are several challenges that complicate patch management. Organizations that do not overcome these challenges will be unable to patch systems effectively and efficiently, leading to compromises that are easily preventable. Organizations that can minimize the time they spend dealing with patching can use those resources for addressing other security concerns. Already many organizations have largely operationalized their patch management, making it more of a core IT function than a part of security. However, it is still important for all organizations to carefully consider patch management in the context of security because patch management is so important to achieving and maintaining sound security.

Patch management is required by various security compliance frameworks, mandates, and other policies. For example, NIST Special Publication (SP) 800-53[2] requires the SI-2, Flaw Remediation security control, which includes installing security-relevant software and firmware patches, testing patches before installing them, and incorporating patches into the organization's configuration management processes. Another example is the Payment Card Industry (PCI) Data Security Standard (DSS)[3], which requires that the latest patches be installed and sets a maximum timeframe for installing the most critical patches.

---

[2] http://csrc.nist.gov/publications/PubsSPs.html#800-53-rev4
[3] https://www.pcisecuritystandards.org/security_standards/

3. The Challenges of Patch Management

This section briefly examines the challenges inherent in performing patch management. These are the challenges that the patch management technologies discussed in Section 4 are trying to solve.

3.1 Timing, Prioritization, and Testing

Timing, prioritization, and testing are intertwined issues for enterprise patch management. Ideally, an organization would deploy every new patch immediately to minimize the time that systems are vulnerable to the associated software flaws. However, in reality this is simply not possible because organizations have limited resources, which makes it necessary to prioritize which patches should be installed before other patches. Further complicating this is the significant risk of installing patches without first testing them, which could cause serious operational disruptions, potentially even more damaging than the corresponding security impact of not pushing the patches out. Unfortunately, testing patches consumes even more of an organization's limited resources and makes patch prioritization even more important. For patch management, timing, prioritization, and testing are often in conflict.

Product vendors have responded to this conflict by improving the quality of their patches and bundling patches for their products. Instead of releasing dozens of patches one at a time over a period of three months, necessitating testing and patch deployment every few days, a vendor might release their patches in a single bundle once a quarter. This allows an organization to perform testing once and roll out patches once, which is far more efficient than testing and rolling out all the patches separately. It also reduces the need to prioritize patches—the organization just needs to prioritize the bundle instead of separately prioritizing each patch it contains. Vendors who bundle patches tend to release them monthly or quarterly, except for cases when an unpatched vulnerability is actively being exploited, in which case they usually issue the appropriate patch immediately instead of delaying it for the next bundle.

There is a downside to patch bundling; it lengthens the time from when a vulnerability is discovered to the time a patch for it becomes publicly available. If an attacker discovers the same vulnerability before the patch is released, the attacker may have a longer window of opportunity to exploit the vulnerability because of the intentional delay in releasing the patch. However, there are two mitigating factors here. One is that if exploitation is known to be occurring, the vendor is likely to release the patch immediately. The other factor is that patches may be installed more quickly if they are bundled than if they are all released separately. So operationally, bundling patches may effectively shrink the window of opportunity for vulnerabilities in some environments.

There are even more issues to consider with timing. The release of a patch may provide attackers with the information that they need to exploit the corresponding vulnerability (e.g., reverse engineer the vulnerability from the patch), meaning that a newly released patch might need to be applied immediately to avoid compromises. However, if a vulnerability is not being exploited yet, organizations should carefully weigh the security risks of not patching with the operational risks of patching without first performing thorough testing. In some operational environments, such as virtual hosts with snapshot capabilities enabled, it may be preferable to patch without testing as long as the organization is fully prepared to roll back the patches if they cause usability or functionality problems.

Another fundamental issue with timing is that to make a patch take effect, it may be necessary to force the implementation of changes; this can require restarting a patched application or service, rebooting the operating system[4], or making other changes to the state of the host. Ultimately what matters is not when the patch was installed, but when the patch actually takes effect. In some cases it may make more sense to mitigate a vulnerability through an alternative method, at least until patches are fully deployed and operational. An example is changing configuration settings for vulnerable software to temporarily block vulnerable application functionality. Each mitigation option has different implications for the security, functionality, and operations of the vulnerable host, so it is not a trivial matter to select one option over others. Also, if configuration settings are changed, this necessitates preserving the old setting values and restoring them at the appropriate time. Another problem with changing configuration settings is that they often require a state change to the host to take effect, such as restarting an application. Implementing configuration changes may be as disruptive to the operations of a host as installing a patch.

Prioritizing which patches to apply and when to apply them is closely related to timing, but there are other considerations as well. It can depend on the relative importance of the vulnerable systems (for example, servers versus clients) and the relative severity of each vulnerability (e.g., vulnerability severity metrics such as the Common Vulnerability Scoring System [CVSS]). Another consideration is dependencies that patches may have on each other; installing one patch may require installing other patches first, and in some cases require restarting an application or rebooting a host multiple times to make the patches take effect sequentially.

In summary, organizations should carefully consider the relevant issues related to timing, prioritization, and testing when planning and executing their enterprise patch management processes.

3.2 Patch Management Configuration

Another major challenge in enterprise patch management is that there are usually multiple mechanisms for applying patches. For example:

- A piece of software may be able to automatically update itself.

- A centralized OS management tool may be able to initiate patching.

- Third-party patch management applications may be able to initiate patching.

- Network access control, health check technologies, and similar technologies may be able to initiate patching.

- A user may be able to manually direct software to update itself.

- A user may be able to manually install a patch or a new version of the software.

Having multiple ways of applying patches can cause conflicts. Multiple methods might each try to patch the same software, which is particularly problematic when the organization doesn't want certain patches applied because of issues with those patches, testing delays, etc. Multiple methods can also cause patches to be delayed or missed because each tool or administrator may assume another one is already taking care of a particular patch. Organizations should identify all the ways in which patches could be applied and act to resolve any conflicts among patch application methods.

---

[4] This can be problematic when the host requires authentication before booting, such as the use of full disk encryption (FDE) software. Organizations using FDE software or other technologies that require authentication before booting should carefully consider the impact that these technologies may have on patch installation.

A related problem with patch management configuration is that users may override or circumvent patch management processes. If users are able to make changes to their hosts' software, such as altering settings (e.g., enabling direct updates, disabling patch management software), installing old versions of software, and uninstalling patches, they can undermine the integrity of the patch management process. To address these problems, organizations should ensure that users cannot disable or otherwise negatively affect enterprise patch management technologies, and organizations should perform continuous monitoring of enterprise patch management technologies to identify any issues that occur.

3.3 Alternative Host Architectures

Enterprise patch management is relatively straightforward when all of the hosts are fully managed and running typical applications and operating systems on a regular platform. When alternative host architectures are employed, patch management can be considerably more challenging. Examples of these architectures include the following:

- **Unmanaged hosts.** As discussed in Section 3.2, it can be much more difficult to control patching when hosts are not centrally managed (i.e., users manage their own hosts).

- **Out-of-office hosts (e.g., telework laptops).** Hosts on other networks are not protected by the enterprise's network security controls (firewalls, network intrusion detection systems, vulnerability scanners, etc.)

- **Non-standard IT components (e.g., appliances).** On such hosts, it's often not possible to patch individual applications independently. Rather, the organization must wait for the component vendor to release updated software. This wait time may be significantly longer than that used by the primary application vendors, resulting in significant vulnerability windows.

- **Mobile devices.** Smartphones, tablets, and other mobile devices (excluding laptops) typically run mobile operating systems, and patching for these devices is fundamentally different. It is often necessary to connect the mobile device to a desktop or laptop and to acquire and download updates through that desktop or laptop. Some mobile devices can directly download updates, but this can be problematic because of bandwidth considerations (such as taking a long time to download large updates and paying data charges for the downloads). Another option for keeping mobile devices updated is the use of enterprise mobile device management software. Enterprise mobile device management software is used to manage mobile devices, even personally owned devices not controlled by the organization. It can install, update, and remove applications, and it can restrict enterprise access if the phone's operating system and mobile device management software are not up to date. See Section 3 of SP 800-124 Revision 1, *Guidelines for Managing and Securing Mobile Devices in the Enterprise*, for more information.

- **Operating system virtualization.** Patches need to be maintained for every OS image and snapshot used for full virtualization. Patching capabilities are often built into virtualized environments, such as the ability to patch offline images and quarantine dormant virtual machine instances. See NIST SP 800-125, *Guide to Security for Full Virtualization Technologies*, for additional information—specifically, Section 3.3 discusses virtual machine image and snapshot management.

- **Firmware.** Firmware updates, such as updating the system BIOS, generally require special privileges and involve different procedures than other types of updates. See NIST SP 800-147, *BIOS Protection Guidelines*, for additional information on BIOS updates.

Organizations should carefully consider all alternative host architectures in use for the enterprise when designing enterprise patch management policies and solutions.

3.4 Other Challenges

This section briefly discusses other challenges not covered earlier in this section. Also, see NIST SP 800-40 Version 2, *Creating a Patch and Vulnerability Management Program* for additional challenges not mentioned in this publication.[5]

3.4.1 Software Inventory Management

Enterprise patch management is dependent on having a current and complete inventory of the patchable software (applications and operating systems) installed on each host. This inventory should include not only which software is currently installed on each host, but also what version of each piece of software is installed. Without this information, the correct patches cannot be identified, acquired, and installed. This inventory information is also necessary for identifying older versions of installed software so that they can be brought up to date. A major benefit of updating older versions is that it reduces the number of software versions that need to be patched and have their patches tested.

3.4.2 Resource Overload

Enterprise patch management can cause resources to become overloaded. For example, many hosts might start downloading the same large patch (or bundle of patches) at the same time. This could consume excessive network bandwidth or, if the patches are coming from an organization patch server, overwhelm the resources of that server. Organizations should ensure that their enterprise patch management can avoid resource overload situations, such as by sizing the solution to meet expected volumes of requests, and staggering the delivery of patches so that the enterprise patch management system does not try to transfer patches to too many hosts at the same time.

3.4.3 Installation Side Effects

Installing a patch may cause side effects to occur. A common example is the installation inadvertently altering existing security configuration settings or adding new settings. This may create a new security problem in the process of fixing the original vulnerability via patching. Organizations should be capable of detecting side effects, such as changes to security configuration settings, caused by patch installation.

3.4.4 Patch Implementation Verification

As discussed in Section 3.1, an installed patch might not take effect until the affected software is restarted or other state changes are made. It can be surprisingly difficult to examine a host and determine whether or not a particular patch has taken effect. This is further complicated when there is no indication for a patch when it would take effect (reboot required/not required, etc.) One option is to attempt to exploit the vulnerability, but this is generally only feasible if an exploit already exists, and there are substantial risks with attempting exploitation, even under highly controlled conditions. Organizations should use other methods of confirming installation, such as a vulnerability scanner that is independent from the patch management system.

---

[5] http://csrc.nist.gov/publications/nistpubs/800-40-Ver2/SP800-40v2.pdf

3.4.5 Application Whitelisting

Application whitelisting technologies can conflict with patch management technologies because the application whitelisting technologies function based on known characteristics of executables and other application components, which may be changed by patching. If the vendor is providing the whitelist information, the vendor will have to acquire the patch, record its files' characteristics, and send the corresponding information to customers. If the organization is building its own whitelist information, it will have to acquire each patch, record its files' characteristics, and update its whitelists with the new information. Either method may cause problematic delays for organizations that apply patches quickly, especially automatically; patched software may be seen as unknown software and thus prohibited from running.

To avoid these problems with updates, most application whitelisting technologies offer maintenance options. For example, many technologies allow the administrator to select certain services (e.g., patch management software) to be trusted updaters. This means that any files that they add to or modify on a host are automatically added to the whitelist. Similar options are available for designating trusted publishers (i.e., software vendors), users (such as system administrators), sources (such as trusted network paths), and other trusted entities that may update whitelists. Organizations using application whitelisting technologies should ensure that they are configured to avoid problems with updates.

4.   Enterprise Patch Management Technologies

This section explores the core concepts of enterprise patch management technologies. It discusses their composition, focuses on the security and management capabilities that they provide, and gives recommendations for their use.

4.1   Components and Architecture

Enterprise patch management technologies are similar architecturally to other enterprise security solutions: one or more centralized servers that provide management and reporting, and one or more consoles.[6] What distinguishes enterprise patch management technologies from each other architecturally are the techniques they use to identify missing patches. The three techniques are agent-based, agentless scanning, and passive network monitoring. Many products support only one of these techniques, while other products support more than one. All the techniques are explained in more detail below. Organizations should carefully consider the advantages and disadvantages of each technique when selecting enterprise patch management technologies.

4.1.1   Agent-Based

An agent-based patch management technology requires an agent to be running on each host to be patched[7], with one or more servers that manage the patching process and coordinate with the agents. Each agent is responsible for determining what vulnerable software is installed on the host, communicating with the patch management servers, determining what new patches are available for the host, installing those patches, and executing any state changes needed to make the patches take effect (e.g., application restart, OS reboot). Each agent runs with administrator privileges so it can perform these actions. The patch management server is responsible for providing the agents with information on vulnerable software and available patches, including where patches can be acquired from and what state changes are needed.

Compared to agentless scanning and passive network monitoring, agent-based patch management technologies are strongly preferred for hosts that are not on the local network all the time, such as telecommuter laptops and smartphones.

There are a few limitations to agent-based patch management technologies. Hosts that don't permit direct administrator access to the operating system, such as many appliances, generally cannot run agents. Also, agents may not be available for all of the organization's platforms, either for technical reasons or operational reasons (such as control systems, medical devices, and other specialized systems).

4.1.2   Agentless Scanning

An agentless scanning patch management technology has one or more servers that perform network scanning of each host to be patched and determine what patches each host needs. Generally agentless scanning requires the servers to have administrative privileges on each host, so that they can return more accurate scanning results and so they have the ability to install patches and implement state changes on the hosts (application restarts, OS reboots, etc.)

The main advantage of agentless scanning is that it doesn't require the installation and execution of an agent on each host.

---

[6]   Enterprise patch management technologies can also be offered as a managed service.
[7]   Agent-based patch management technology is built into some operating systems.

One of the primary limitations of agentless scanning is that it omits hosts not on the local network, such as telecommuter laptops and mobile devices. Also, network security controls (e.g., host-based firewalls) and network technologies (e.g., network address translation) may inadvertently block scanning or otherwise negatively affect scanning results. Agentless scanning may also negatively impact operations by consuming excessive amounts of bandwidth. Finally, agentless scanning may not support all of the organization's platforms.

4.1.3 Passive Network Monitoring

Passive network monitoring technologies for patch management monitor local network traffic to identify applications (and in some cases, operating systems) that are in need of patching.

These technologies can be effective at identifying hosts that are not being maintained by other patch management solutions (agent-based, agentless scanning). They do not require any privileges on the hosts to be monitored, so they can be used to monitor the patch status of hosts that the organization does not control (unmanaged systems, visitor systems, contractor systems, etc.)

The primary disadvantage of passive network monitoring is that it only works with software where you can identify the version based on its network traffic (assumed to be unencrypted). Also, of course, it only works with hosts on the local network.

4.1.4 Comparison of Techniques

Table 4-1 summarizes the major characteristics of the three techniques.

Table 4-1: Comparison of Techniques

Characteristic	Agent-Based	Agentless Scanning	Passive Network Monitoring
Admin privileges needed on hosts?	Yes	Yes	No
Supports unmanaged hosts?	No	No	Yes
Supports remote hosts?	Yes	No	No
Supports appliances?	No	No	Yes
Bandwidth needed for scanning?	Minimal	Moderate to excessive	None
Potential range of applications detected?	Comprehensive	Comprehensive	Only those that generate unencrypted network traffic

4.2 Security Capabilities

This section describes common security capabilities provided by patch management technologies, divided into three categories: inventory management, patch management, and other. In many products these capabilities are provided by using the Security Content Automation Protocol (SCAP). SCAP is designed to organize, express, and measure security-related information in standardized ways. See Appendix A for more information on SCAP and its role in patch management.

4.2.1 Inventory Management Capabilities

Patch management technologies typically have capabilities for identifying which software and versions of software are installed on each host, or alternately, just identifying vulnerable versions of software that are installed. In addition, some products have features for installing new versions of software, installing or uninstalling software features, and uninstalling software.

4.2.2 Patch Management Capabilities

Patch management technologies obviously provide a range of patch management capabilities. Common features include identifying which patches are needed, bundling and sequencing patches for distribution, allowing administrators to select which patches may or may not be deployed, and installing patches and verifying installation. Many patch management technologies also allow patches to be stored centrally (within the organization) or downloaded as needed from external sources.

4.2.3 Other Capabilities

Many host-based products that have patch management capabilities also provide a variety of other security capabilities, such as antivirus software, configuration management, and vulnerability scanning. Further discussion of these capabilities is outside the scope of this document.

4.3 Management Capabilities

Once a patch management technology has been selected, its administrators should design a solution architecture, perform testing, deploy and secure the solution, and maintain its operations and security. This section highlights issues of particular interest with administration—implementation, operation, and maintenance—of patch management technologies, and provides recommendations for performing them effectively and efficiently.

4.3.1 Technology Security

Deploying enterprise patch management tools within an enterprise can create additional security risks for an organization; however, a much greater risk is faced by organizations that do not effectively patch their systems. Such tools usually increase security far more than they decrease security, especially when the tools contain built-in security measures to protect against security risks and threats. The following are some risks with using these tools:

- A patch may have been altered (inadvertently or intentionally).

- Credentials may be misused.

- Vulnerabilities in the solution components (including agents) may be exploited.

- An entity could monitor tool communications to identify vulnerabilities (particularly when the host is on an external network).

Organizations should reduce these risks through the application of standard security techniques that should be used when deploying any enterprise-wide application. Examples of countermeasures include the following:

- Keep the patching solution components tightly secured (including patching them).

- Encrypt network communications.

10

■ Verify integrity of patches before installing them (e.g., using checksums).

■ Test patches before deployment (to identify corruption).

4.3.2 Phased Deployment

Organizations should deploy enterprise patch management tools using a phased approach. This allows process and user communication issues to be addressed with a small group before deploying the patch application universally. Most organizations deploy patch management tools first to standardized desktop systems and single-platform server farms of similarly configured servers. Once this has been accomplished, organizations should address the more difficult issue of integrating multiplatform environments, nonstandard desktop systems, legacy computers, and computers with unusual configurations. Manual methods may need to be used for operating systems and applications not supported by automated patching tools, as well as some computers with unusual configurations; examples include embedded systems, industrial control systems, medical devices, and experimental systems. For such computers, there should be a written and implemented procedure for the manual patching process.

4.3.3 Usability and Availability

Organizations should balance their security needs with their needs for usability and availability. For example, installing a patch may "break" other applications; this can best be addressed by testing patches before deployment. Another example is that forcing application restarts, OS reboots, and other host state changes is disruptive and could cause loss of data or services. Again, organizations need to balance the need to get patches applied with the need to support operations. A final example, particularly important for mobile devices, is the acquisition of updates over low-bandwidth or metered connections; it may be technically or financially infeasible to download large patches over such connections. Organizations should make provisions for ensuring that their enterprise patching solution works for mobile hosts and other hosts used on low-bandwidth or metered networks.

5.   Metrics

As explained in Section 3.3 of NIST SP 800-55 Revision 1, *Performance Measurement Guide for Information Security* there are three types of measures:

- "Implementation measures are used to demonstrate progress in implementing security programs, specific security controls, and associated policies and procedures....

- Effectiveness/efficiency measures are used to monitor if program-level processes and system-level security controls are implemented correctly, operating as intended, and meeting the desired outcome....

- Impact measures are used to articulate the impact of information security on an organization's mission...."

Regarding these types of measures, "less mature information security programs need to develop their goals and objectives before being able to implement effective measurement. More mature programs use implementation measures to evaluate performance, while the most mature programs use effectiveness/efficiency and business impact measures to determine the effect of their information security processes and procedures." Accordingly, organizations should implement and use appropriate measures for their enterprise patch management technologies and processes.

Examples of possible implementation measures include:

- What percentage of the organization's desktops and laptops are being covered by the enterprise patch management technologies?

- What percentage of the organization's servers have their applications automatically inventoried by the enterprise patch management technologies?

Examples of possible effectiveness/efficiency measures include:

- How often are hosts checked for missing updates?

- How often are asset inventories for host applications updated?

- What is the minimum/average/maximum time to apply patches to X% of hosts?

- What percentage of the organization's desktops and laptops are patched within X days of patch release? Y days? Z days? (where X, Y, and Z are different values, such as 10, 20, and 30)

- On average, what percentage of hosts are fully patched at any given time? Percentage of high impact hosts? Moderate impact? Low impact?

- What percentage of patches are applied fully automatically, versus partially automatically, versus manually?

Examples of possible impact measures include:

- What cost savings has the organization achieved through its patch management processes?

- What percentage of the agency's information system budget is devoted to patch management?

Appendix A—Security Content Automation Protocol (SCAP) Tutorial

This appendix provides an overview of the Security Content Automation Protocol (SCAP) as it relates to enterprise patch management technologies. The appendix is based on material from NIST SP 800-117 Revision 1, *Guide to Adopting and Using the Security Content Automation Protocol (SCAP) Version 1.2*, which is the current revision as of this writing. Please see the current revision of NIST SP 800-117 for additional information on SCAP.

SCAP (pronounced ess-cap), as expressed in NIST Special Publication (SP) 800-126, is "a suite of specifications that standardize the format and nomenclature by which software flaw and security configuration information is communicated, both to machines and humans." SCAP is designed to organize, express, and measure security-related information in standardized ways, as well as related reference data, such as identifiers for software flaws and security configuration issues. SCAP can be used to maintain the security of enterprise systems, such as automatically verifying the installation of patches, checking system security configuration settings, and examining systems for signs of compromise.

Table A-1 lists the component specifications for the SCAP version 1.2 protocol. The components are grouped by type:

- **Languages.** The SCAP languages provide standard vocabularies and conventions for expressing security policy, technical check mechanisms, and assessment results.

- **Reporting formats.** The SCAP reporting formats provide the necessary constructs to express collected information in standardized formats.

- **Enumerations**. Each SCAP enumeration defines a standard nomenclature (naming format) and an official dictionary or list of items expressed using that nomenclature.

- **Measurement and scoring systems.** In SCAP this refers to evaluating specific characteristics of a security weakness (for example, software vulnerabilities and security configuration issues) and, based on those characteristics, generating a score that reflects their relative severity.

- **Integrity protection.** An SCAP integrity protection specification helps to preserve the integrity of SCAP content and results.

Table A-1. SCAP Version 1.2 Component Specifications

SCAP Component	Description
Languages	
Extensible Configuration Checklist Description Format (XCCDF) 1.2	A language for authoring security checklists/benchmarks and for reporting results of evaluating them
Open Vulnerability and Assessment Language (OVAL) 5.10	A language for representing system configuration information, assessing machine state, and reporting assessment results
Open Checklist Interactive Language (OCIL) 2.0	A language for representing assessment content that collects information from people or from existing data stores made by other data collection efforts
Reporting Formats	
Asset Reporting Format (ARF) 1.2	A format for expressing the exchange of information about assets and the relationships between assets and reports
Asset Identification	A format for uniquely identifying assets based on known identifiers and/or known information about the assets

SCAP Component	Description
Enumerations	
Common Platform Enumeration (CPE) 2.3	A nomenclature and dictionary of hardware, operating systems, and applications, plus an applicability language for constructing complex logical groupings of CPE names
Common Configuration Enumeration (CCE) 5	A nomenclature and dictionary of software security configurations
Common Vulnerabilities and Exposures (CVE)	A nomenclature and dictionary of security-related software flaws
Measurement and Scoring Systems	
Common Vulnerability Scoring System (CVSS) 2.0	A system for measuring the relative severity of software flaw vulnerabilities
Common Configuration Scoring System (CCSS) 1.0	A system for measuring the relative severity of system security configuration issues
Integrity Protection	
Trust Model for Security Automation Data (TMSAD) 1.0	A specification for using digital signatures in a common trust model applied to other security automation specifications

Each of the SCAP components offers unique functions and can be used independently, but greater benefits can be achieved by using the components together. For example, the ability to have XCCDF documents that use CCE, CPE, and CVE identifiers with OVAL definitions to express rules and relationships for technical checks and that use OCIL questionnaires to express management and operational checks comprises the building blocks for *SCAP-expressed* checklists.[8] In other words, SCAP-expressed checklists use a standardized language (XCCDF) to express what checks should be performed (OVAL, OCIL), which platforms are being discussed (CPE), and which security settings (CCE) and software flaw vulnerabilities (CVE) should be addressed.

Both comprehensive SCAP-expressed checklists, such as a checklist to secure an operating system, and more specialized SCAP-expressed checklists are valuable. A specialized checklist can be used to check particular characteristics of systems to identify potential security problems. A common example is using an SCAP checklist to confirm the installation of patches and identify which patches are missing. SCAP-formatted data for patch checking can be made publicly available by software vendors for their products; organizations can download this data and use it through their SCAP-capable tools.[9]

---

[8] SCAP-expressed checklists are further defined in Table 4-1 of NIST SP 800-70 Revision 1.
[9] Patch information can be downloaded from the MITRE OVAL Repository at http://oval.mitre.org/repository/.

Appendix B—Summary of Recommendations

This appendix provides a summary of the main recommendations made throughout the publication.

Section 3

Section 3.1: If a vulnerability is not being exploited yet, organizations should carefully weigh the security risks of not patching with the operational risks of patching without performing thorough testing first.

Section 3.1: Organizations should carefully consider the relevant issues related to timing, prioritization, and testing when planning and executing their enterprise patch management processes.

Section 3.2: Organizations should identify all the ways in which patches could be applied and act to resolve any conflicts among patch application methods.

Section 3.2: Organizations should ensure that users cannot disable or otherwise negatively affect enterprise patch management technologies, and organizations should perform continuous monitoring of enterprise patch management technologies to identify any issues that occur.

Section 3.3: Organizations should carefully consider all alternative host architectures in use for the enterprise when designing enterprise patch management policies and solutions.

Section 3.4.1: The inventory of the patchable software (applications and operating systems) installed on each host should include not only which software is currently installed on each host, but also what version of each piece of software is installed.

Section 3.4.2: Organizations should ensure that their enterprise patch management can avoid resource overload situations.

Section 3.4.3: Organizations should be capable of detecting side effects, such as changes to security configuration settings, caused by patch installation.

Section 3.4.4: Organizations should use other methods of confirming installation, such as a vulnerability scanner that is independent from the patch management system.

Section 3.4.5: Organizations using application whitelisting technologies should ensure that they are configured to avoid problems with updates.

Section 4

Section 4.1: Organizations should carefully consider the advantages and disadvantages of each technique for identifying missing patches (e.g., agent-based, agentless scanning, passive network monitoring) when selecting enterprise patch management technologies.

Section 4.3: A patch management technology's administrators should design a solution architecture, perform testing, deploy and secure the solution, and maintain its operations and security.

Section 4.3.1: Organizations should reduce the risks of using enterprise patch management tools through the application of standard security techniques that should be used when deploying any enterprise-wide application.

Section 4.3.2: Organizations should deploy enterprise patch management tools using a phased approach.

Section 4.3.3: Organizations should balance their security needs with their needs for usability and availability.

Section 5

Section 5: Organizations should implement and use appropriate measures for their enterprise patch management technologies and processes.

Appendix C—Acronyms and Abbreviations

Selected acronyms and abbreviations used in the guide are defined below.

ARF	Asset Reporting Format
CCE	Common Configuration Enumeration
CCSS	Common Configuration Scoring System
CPE	Common Platform Enumeration
CVE	Common Vulnerabilities and Exposures
CVSS	Common Vulnerability Scoring System
FISMA	Federal Information Security Management Act
IT	Information Technology
ITL	Information Technology Laboratory
NIST	National Institute of Standards and Technology
OCIL	Open Checklist Interactive Language
OMB	Office of Management and Budget
OVAL	Open Vulnerability and Assessment Language
SCAP	Security Content Automation Protocol
SP	Special Publication
TMSAD	Trust Model for Security Automation Data
XCCDF	Extensible Configuration Checklist Description Format